Animals on Our Farm

Julie Haydon

Contents

Our Farm

My home is on a big farm.
We have lots of animals
on our farm.

Sheep

We have sheep on our farm.

Sheep have **wool**.

You can make things with wool.

My hat is made of wool.

Chickens

We have chickens
on our farm.
Chickens lay eggs.

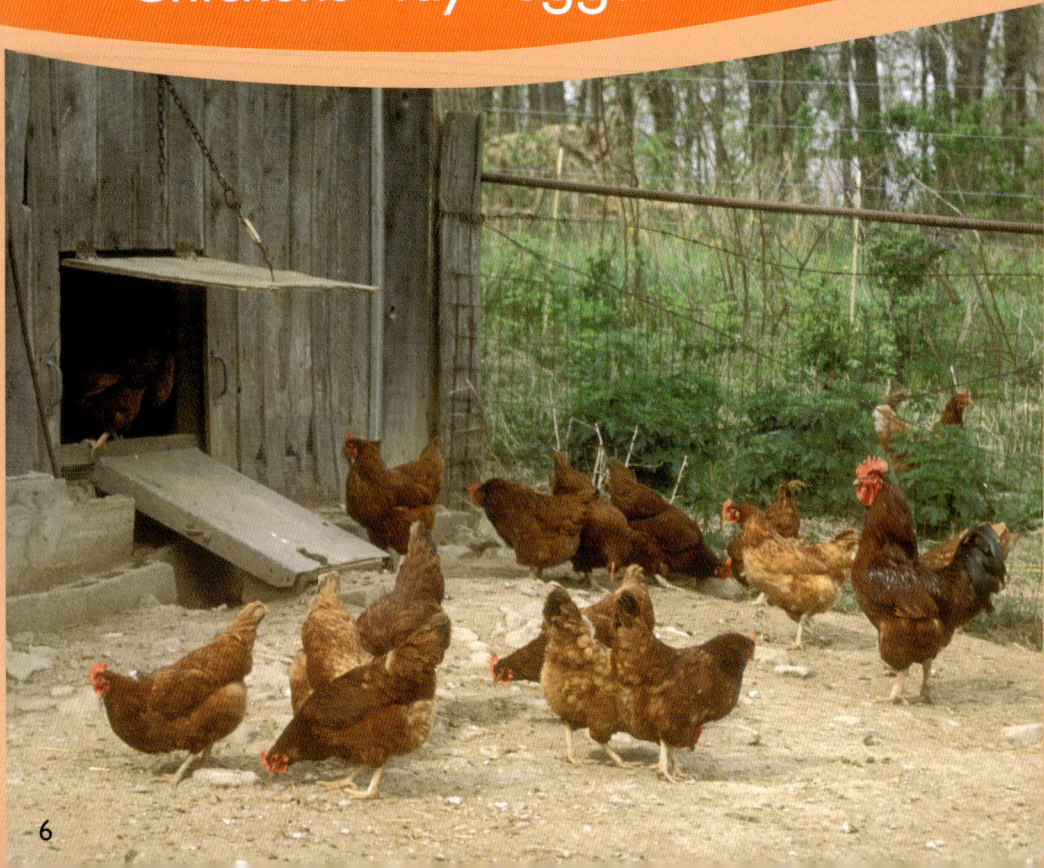

You can eat eggs.

I like eggs for breakfast.

Cows

We have cows on our farm.

Cows make milk.

You can drink milk.
You can eat foods
made with milk.

I like cheese.
Cheese is made with milk.

Dogs

We have dogs on our farm.
The dogs help
with the sheep.

Horses

We have horses on our farm.
The horses are for riding.

My Pets

Some of the animals
on our farm are pets.

This is my dog, Digger.
I play with Digger.

This is my cat, Moon.

I like to play with Moon, too.

Our Animals

Our animals have food and water.

We look after our animals.

I like all the animals
on our farm.
But I like Digger
and Moon best.

Glossary

wool